DARTMOOR

by ROY WESTLAKE ARPS   text by CRISPIN GILL

David & Charles

Newton Abbot   London   North Pomfret (Vt)

DEDICATION

In memory of William Crossing
– the first Dartmoor enthusiast –
and to all lovers of the moor

*' Those who have once set foot upon Dartmoor, who have
climbed its giant tors, have listened to the plaintive music
of its streams or have passed into its solitary places,
where the cry of the curlew alone is heard, will,
if they be true lovers of Nature,
ever feel a longing to revisit it.'*

WILLIAM CROSSING: *Gems in a Granite Setting*

British Library Cataloguing in Publication Data
Westlake, Roy
 Dartmoor.
 1. Dartmoor (England) – Description and travel – Guide-books
 I. Title II. Gill, Crispin
 914.23'5304858   DA670.D2

 ISBN 0-7153-9079-1

The text in the first section of this book first appeared in *Dartmoor* in the
David and Charles Leisure and Travel Series, now out of print. Where necessary it is revised
and updated

© Photographs: Roy Westlake 1987 © Text: Crispin Gill 1987
© Text for 'Photography on Dartmoor': Roy Westlake 1987

Designed by John Youé & Associates. Colour origination by Columbia, Singapore. Typeset by Typesetters (Birmingham) Ltd, Smethwick, West Midlands
Printed & bound in West Germany by Mohndruck GmbH
for David & Charles Publishers plc Brunel House Newton Abbot Devon

Published in the United States of America by David & Charles Inc North Pomfet Vermont 05053 USA

Contents

The Legendary Land   4

The Making of Dartmoor   6

Man on the Moor   8

Weather and Wildlife   12

The Motorist's Moor   14

The Walker's Moor   16

The Wooded Valleys   22

The North and South Moor   26

Map of Dartmoor   29

Appendices: 30

   1   Military Range Danger Area
   2   Peat Passes in Northern Dartmoor
   3   Dartmoor Letter Boxes
   4   Heights of some Dartmoor Hills
   5   Dartmoor National Park

FRONT COVER
This old cross overlooks Foxtor Mires on the Southern moor.

BACK COVER
Leather Tor, looking towards Sheep's Tor.

TITLE PAGE
Dartmoor ponies, free to wander, capture the feeling of freedom on the open moor.

RIGHT
Walker on a moorland track.

The Legendary Land

There was no road across Dartmoor until 200 years ago. Then the turnpike makers in their new zeal drove a metalled road from Tavistock to Moretonhampstead, and later added spurs from Two Bridges to Yelverton and Ashburton. No roads crossing the Moor from side to side have been added since, and only two settlements, Princetown and Postbridge, have grown up beside these roads. There were, and are, villages and hamlets round the edge of the Moor; but with the exception of the Ancient Tenements in the three main valleys of the Dart, there were no settlements over the 1,000ft contour. The roads brought in the improvers who enclosed thousands of acres and created new farms; today they are little more than stone walls.

Even today, on a tarred road marked with cat's eyes and in a snug modern motor car, it can be a hair-raising operation to cross the Moor at night in fog or a gale of wind and rain. Before the roads were made the only guide was the turf worn by the feet of previous tavellers with an occasional stone cross or marking stone, easily missed, to show the way. 'It was most perilous for the traveller', wrote Mrs Bray in 1832; 'for if he missed his line of direction, or became entangled amidst rocks or marshy grounds, or was enveloped in one of those frequent mists here so much to be dreaded, that prevented him even from seeing the course of the sun above his head . . . he was likely to be lost on the moor, and, in the depth of winter, to be frozen to death, as many there have been.'

Dartmoor was a place to be avoided unless there were grazing animals to be tended, or peat to be cut, or whortleberries gathered, or employment found in a mine. Even the mineworkers camped out; an old man still living in Meavy worked as a boy sharpening tools for the Hexworthy miners. He walked out across the southern Moor at dawn of a Monday with his food for the week, and home again on the Saturday evening. In the 1930s an old farmer inquired in the Royal Oak 'What's it like to Dartymoor? I never bin there.' Yet he had lived in Meavy with the Moor all round him all his life.

The Moor held its terrors. Dewer the black huntsman, the Devil himself, hunted all night across its desolation with a pack of black hell hounds, riding west as the eastern sky lightened until, as the sun broke over the eastern horizon, he leaped from the summit of the Dewerstone out into the still-dark west. A farmer riding fuddled home from market met Dewer one night. Full of Dutch courage he called 'What sport, huntsman?' 'Good sport', answered the hunter and flung a warm bundle to the farmer. He rested it across his saddlebow and rode on, calling for a light as he clattered into his farmyard. His wife ran out holding a lantern high and there in its light, across the farmer's knees, was the body of their recently-born baby. The folklore of all Europe has the devil hunting, and black hounds, but in all wild places the eerie quality of the wilderness, the unknown land, is ascribed to old Nick. He was a familiar figure; after he finished building Brentor Church (the monks tried to build it on top of the tor and each night he cast it down, so they built it at the foot of the tor and he put it on top) he called at the Tavistock Inn, Poundsgate, for a pint. The customers knew it was the Devil because his ale boiled as it reached his lips, and his pot burnt a circular mark on the bar when he put it down.

'They'm piskies up to Dartymoor . . .'

Pixies today are only tawdry figures to mislead the tourists. But those who walk in a circle in fog are pixie-led (turn your coat inside-out to defeat them), and a child with pointed ears is a changeling. There has been an attempt to explain the Dartmoor pixie belief. Although there is no evidence of settled habitation on Dartmoor between about 400 BC and the coming of the Saxons about AD 700, there are a few surviving place names with the 'Wal' element (as in Wales and Cornwall) which suggests the older race, strangers to the Saxons. As these newcomers pushed their farms up into the Moor, were there still colonies of these small dark people there, living in their turf huts? A dwindling race, moving back into inhospitable land, were they driven to steal the odd animal, or bowl of milk, from the newcomers; even, when their own children had died, to steal a child that their race might survive? Did they wear rough clothes bright with natural dyes? And if, stealthily followed by the rare, scared observer venturing into unknown high ground, did they not seem to disappear on the hillside when in fact they had entered their hut, made of the same stone and turf as the Moor itself? Who would dare venture further?

Nonsense now, of course, but not everyone can find the pixie's cave on Sheepstor. Those who do leave at least a pin, or something for the pixies, but they never find anything that they or anyone else has left before. When the medieval travellers who ventured across the Moor set up tall marker stones to define the route, they carved those stones into Christian crosses.

Dartmoor is not just the last wilderness in southern England, it is a territory that has only been lightly inhabited at any time in history. It has the wisht, fey quality of loneliness and isolation which can stimulate the mind to recall the old stories, even the old gods and the old devils. For modern man, the true adventure of Dartmoor is setting out alone into high, empty country. An expedition into Dartmoor can be real exploration, meeting as much challenge as one cares to set.

The view from Combestone Tor, near Hexworthy, is magnificent. Here we are looking along the Dart Valley towards Dartmeet.

The Making of Dartmoor

Between 400 and 300 million years ago that part of the earth's surface we now know as Devon and Cornwall lay quietly under the sea. Alluvial deposits on the bed of that sea made the rocks that now cover much of the area, the shillety Devonian, the carboniferous, the red sandstone. Coral reefs grew, to turn in time into limestone ridges. Then, under pressures from the south, this seabed was pushed up into a fold running roughly east-west. The top of the fold was not even but would have looked like the knuckles of a clenched fist held at eye level. Into the hollow under that fold rushed volcanic material which did not burst the surface but filled the space, moulding itself to the underside of the sedimentary rocks and cooling to become granite.

In the 290 million years or so since that happened the sea level has varied from 2,000ft or more higher than it is now, to 200ft or perhaps more lower. That land has suffered erosion under the sea, been cut into at different levels by the waves, been worn by wind and rain and frost, affected by climates sometimes tropical, sometimes sub-Arctic. Water, air and the rocks themselves have all produced chemicals which eroded them in other ways. On the knuckles the older rocks wore through completely to leave the granite protruding, and these knuckles became the granite bosses that make the backbone of Devon and Cornwall; Dartmoor, Bodmin Moor, the china clay area north of St Austell, the mining country of the Helston-Redruth-Falmouth triangle, West Penwith and the Isles of Scilly. Of these granite areas Dartmoor is the most easterly, the highest, and the largest in area.

But the granite varies. That which cooled against the envelope of older rocks absorbed varying masses of those rocks. All of it in cooling developed long cracks running parallel with the envelope or at right angles to it. Into this shrinking mass came a later intrusion of granite. Once exposed to the elements these different kinds of granite eroded at different rates, and in different ways. Some decomposed into clay and sand to be carried away by rivers or to form the areas being quarried for china clay today. As the surface of the Moor wore down, so harder masses of granite were left standing, to form what we now call tors.

Even before these tors emerged above the neighbouring surface there had been chemical action which removed the material in the faults, so that some tors look like a giant child's heap of bricks. This process was continued by wind, rain and frost; some tors have their hearts eaten out to look like man-made castles. On others, the rocks fragmented, rolling down the sides to make a mass of boulders or 'clitter' – the Dartmoor word for these loose stones – moving away down the hill.

In the last Ice Age the glacial sheet never reached Dartmoor but conditions there were still sub-Arctic. The surface would have frozen deep in the winters, half-melted in the short summers so that whole masses of semi-frozen soil could slip away down the slopes.

Because Dartmoor did not have glaciers there are no ice-gouged valleys with moraines at their foot to make the natural lakes of the other highland areas of Britain; Dartmoor has no natural lakes. But the rivers played their part in shaping the land. Originally the land was tilted to the east, which is the way the moorland Dart and Teign still flow. Then came a second tilt, to the south, and the Dart which had originally flowed out through what is now the Teign estuary cut a new channel south-east from Holne. This second tilt is also the reason why the Dart has long tributaries from the north, but only very short ones from the south. It also accounts for the secondary river system of the Moor: the Plym, Yealm, Erme and Avon, all rising in the southern Moor and flowing to the south. The varying heights of the sea have also affected the river valleys. When the sea level was high – at one time Dartmoor itself was an island – the rivers had not far to go and formed wide valleys in the high Moor with large flood plains. With the sea level low the rivers had a greater fall and cut deep secondary valleys in their old wide courses and steep-sided gorges through the moorland edges to the country below.

First trees, then peat

After the last Ice Age Dartmoor enjoyed a warmer climate from about 3000 BC onwards. First hazel and then oak and elm covered much of the Moor, creating a forest soil. Then about 500 BC the climate became colder and wetter, the forests were destroyed and sank into the soil, to form the peat bogs which still give much of Dartmoor its black acid soil. While it yields little or no grazing it serves as a sponge to hold the rainfall, releasing its water slowly to keep the Dartmoor rivers flowing right through the seasons.

Dartmoor is the worn-down stump of a mountain in the heart of Devon, a far from level plateau which had been likened to an inverted saucer because the highest tors are ranged round its edge, a wilderness of thin grazing. Its rivers tend to descend in steps across the Moor before cutting out of its fastness in dramatic gorges to the pastoral lands below. It is 20 miles across from north to south and almost that distance from east to west; most of it is over a thousand feet above sea level and one little ridge in the north-west corner, from Yes Tor to High Willhays, is over 2,000 feet. The highest point in England south of Kinder Scout (2,088ft) in the Peak District of Derbyshire is High Willhays, at 2,038ft.

One of the many rock faces of Vixen Tor,
near Merrivale.

Man on the Moor

The first men of whom we have any record reached Dartmoor in the days of the great forest. A solitary flint axe found on Brent Moor suggests a hunting expedition by Early Stone Age people of the type who lived in Kent's Cavern at Torquay and other limestone caves, of south Devon. Surface scatterings of flints found beside springs, notably in the Gidleigh-Throwleigh area and as far into the Moor as Postbridge, are taken as evidence of Mesolithic men who made temporary camps in the forest in pursuit of its rich game. They were followed by New Stone Age men of the Neolithic period who had knowledge of farming but seem to have used Dartmoor for hunting forays only.

Various barrows and kistvaens, however, have produced evidence that the Beaker Folk, the early men of the Bronze Age, buried their dead on the Moor, and many of the stone rows and stone circles are believed to be remains of their ceremonial monuments, but again nothing has been found in any settlement to suggest that they lived there. The great problem of all Dartmoor archaeology is that the acid soil destroys most of the clues that men leave behind them; their bones (unless burned), metal, wood, leather; even pottery is weakened. Not until the Bronze Age proper, from about 2000 BC onwards, can pottery finds be accepted as evidence that man lived on the Moor. On the wetter south and western slopes there are some villages in which the houses are in or against the wall of a large pound into which the animals were driven for safety from wild beasts, or else there are groups of huts with no pound. These people seem to have been mainly stock-brreders. On the drier south-eastern and eastern slopes is a third type of village, groups of houses with small square fields. Here growing crops was the major part of the farming, though there were animals as well.

With the deteriorating climate, the fires of the Stone Age hunters and the farming of the Bronze Age men, the forests had been cleared from all but the valley bottoms. Farming spread and continued into the Iron Age, when better tools facilitated both tree-felling and ploughing. Artifacts show a continuation of occupation up to about 400 BC and then there is a break. It would seem that the weather, getting colder and wetter, drove these farmers off the Moor at about that time, and archaeologists talk of a depopulation from about 400 BC until the arrival of the Anglo-Saxons soon after AD 700.

By this time there are scanty written records to help. It is generally accepted that the Saxons had overrun all Devon by AD 710, and that soon after their first settlers moved on to the Moor, above the tangled woods and swamps of the valleys and up to the 1,000ft contour. But they used Celtic names for the rivers – we still do – and that 'wal' prefix in some place names suggests that there were some survivors from earlier times.

Somewhere about AD 900 the Saxon kings made all this Dartmoor heartland a royal hunting ground, and it is argued by W. G. Hoskins that they had their main lodge at Walkhampton, on the western side. When the Normans arrived they made all Dartmoor a formal royal hunting ground, a 'forest', and very soon after applied their strict forest laws to all Devon. Not until 1204 did King John disafforest Devon, apart from Dartmoor, and in 1239 Henry III gave Dartmoor to his brother Richard, Earl of Cornwall. A year later a party of knights made a perambulation, laying down the boundaries that still define the Forest part of the Duchy of Cornwall to this day. Since the Black Prince was made Duke of Cornwall in 1337 the title has always been held by the Sovereign's eldest son: when there is no son the estates are held by the Crown.

In spite of its emptiness and its royal status Dartmoor was not unused. It served as a summer grazing ground for all Devon, and all the people of Devon still have rights there, except the inhabitants of Totnes and Barnstaple. These are the oldest boroughs in the county, but because their early charters did not mention the Dartmoor rights they were held to have forfeited them when they acquired borough rights.

By the eleventh century farms were being established above the 1,000ft contour, but these had all been abandoned by about 1300. Life there may have been too arduous, or even discouraged; of the 100 abandoned settlements that have been located none are actually in the Forest. But about the time the Forest was given to the Earldom of Cornwall there was encouragement to settlement in the Forest itself, in the higher valleys of the Dart, and the 'Ancient Tenements' make their appearance. Of these farms Babeny and Pizwell are mentioned by 1260; there were seventeen of them named by 1563 and all but two are still farmed. The Forest was, and is, part of the manor of Lydford, which meant that these new farmers had to cross the heart of Dartmoor to reach their parish church. To carry the dead a dozen miles across the top of the Moor for burial was a near impossibility in winter, and in 1260 the petition of the Ancient Tenements to use Widecombe Church was granted.

But it was tin and wool, nor farming, that made Widecombe Church 'the Cathedral of the Moor'. Tin was being worked at Brisworthy and Sheepstor, in the Plym and Meavy valleys, by 1156 and for the last quarter of that century southern Dartmoor, between the Plym and the Dart, was the major source in Europe of this vital metal, producing between 300 and 400 tons a year. It was a royal metal from which the King took rich pickings, and in return the miners were virtually above the law, answerable only to their own court for all but crimes like murder and theft of land. They could search for tin where they would, and paid no tolls or taxes other than that on the metal itself.

In 1305 Tavistock, Chagford and Ashburton were made stannary towns (*stannum* is Latin for tin) and Plympton in 1328 made a fourth. All Devon was divided into four stannary areas and all tin had to be taken to its particular town at fixed intervals where royal officers tested and weighed it, and extracted the royal toll.

The tin miners

The first tin was found in the bed of rivers, washed down from higher lodes. Then the miners moved from streaming to digging out the banks, and the broad U-shaped valleys they made can easily be recognised; there is a notable example in Greenwell Gert at the top of Shadycombe, due east of Clearbrook. The piles of pebbles they discarded can be recognised, for example, half a mile above Cadover Bridge on the Plym. The tinners worked up the valleys and, when they were exhausted, adits (narrow shafts) were driven into the sides of the valley. The boom time was up to 1300, with another spurt in Elizabethan times, almost complete cessation by 1750, and then a revival after 1800 when the price of tin rocketed. Deep shafts came in with the nineteenth century and the last mine, at Hexworthy, stopped work in 1914. Apart from the marks of the tin streamers the remains of blowing houses, rough rectangular buildings built into banks beside the streams, where the tin was smelted, can be found. There is a good example on the Walkham, just above Merrivale Bridge. The later miners used much water power to drive their machinery and the leats they built to take water where it was needed, sometimes running for miles along the hillsides, are often still in use.

Apart from tin, lead and silver were mined at Wheal Betsy, whose engine house and chimney are still prominent just east of the Mary Tavy-Lydford road. There was iron at Haytor close to the Rock Inn, copper and arsenic near Sticklepath with slag heaps still beside the A30 road, and a rich complex of copper mines round Tavistock.

Dartmoor was also (and still is) good sheep country and its coarse short wool was important when the wool trade was the staple of England's medieval trade. The Cistercian monks of Buckfast Abbey ran their flocks on Holne, Buckfast and Brent Moors and their brother Cistercians of Buckland Abbey owned much of the south-west Moor. The Benedictines of Tavistock owed much of their wealth to wool sales. Moretonhampstead had a tucking mill (where the cloth was hammered to felt and shrink it) by the end of the thirteenth century and Ashburton had a mill soon after. Tavistock serges were marketed under the town's name and by Tudor times kept fifteen mills busy. There were in fact tucking mills all round the

The restored engine house of Wheal Betsy silver-lead mine on Black Down, in a desolate setting.

9

Moor, and wool remained important through the dog days of tin mining and even after its last boom, though only with blankets coming from Buckfastleigh into our own times.

Leats and waterwheels powered the industry and the mills in their time turned to grinding corn or making edge tools as the market demanded. The mill at Sticklepath, which has been restored to working order, demonstrates the variety of machinery which could be waterpowered.

What really opened up Dartmoor was the building of roads. The Tavistock-Moretonhampstead turnpike was made in 1772 and the Two Bridges-Ashburton road soon after. Some of the Ancient Tenements, which over the centuries had added small 'newtakes' to their original holdings, were taken over by rich men who made them the bases for vast enclosures: there was even in 1791 a plan to enclose the whole Moor. Thomas Tyrwhitt, private secretary to the Prince of Wales, was already building Tor Royal into an estate of 2,300 acres and a little village, Princetown, began to grow at his lodge gates. Then at his suggestion a prison was built on the other side of Princetown to take the French prisoners-of-war overcrowded in the hulks at Plymouth; they arrived in 1809. The prison led to another road being built, from Yelverton to Princetown, in 1812, and when with the end of the war the prison was abandoned in 1816, Tyrwhitt had new ideas. His plan that the desert should bloom like the rose led to a railway, with horses as motive power, linking Plymouth and Princetown by 1823; lime would come up to fertilise the land and the crops and granite would go down. King Tor and Foggin Tor quarries had been opened to build the prison and the railway wound through this still-dramatic complex. But the land did not bloom, the railway was always in financial trouble, and even a scheme to make naphtha in the prison buildings from peat – which had for centuries given fuel to the farmers and tinners – did not work. Then, in 1850, the prison became a convict establishment and has housed civilian criminals ever since.

The enclosures went on through the century; between 1820 and 1898 it was estimated that 15,000 acres had been walled off. So vast blocks on either side of the main roads through the Forest are enclosed, though the land has been so little 'improved' that much is indistinguishable from the open Moor. In addition a number of new farms were made, like Fox Tor and Nun's Cross, but quite a few of these are now abandoned or used as adventure training centres. Farming is still the main occupation on the Moor, with the better grassland cut for hay. Herds of South Devon and Galloway cattle and flocks of grey-faced Dartmoor sheep in the border parishes, Dartmoor white-faced on the Moor with Scottish breeds like Blackface and Cheviot, are the mainstay. In addition most farmers have a few ponies, descendants of the feral Celtic ponies. Though they run wild for most of the year, the ponies are all marked and at the annual round-ups the new colts are identified through their mares and marked before going to market or being returned to the Moor.

In isolated parts of the Moor, away from the farms, warrens were made, artificial banks of earth and stone in which rabbits could breed. In the Plym valley Trowlesworthy was established by 1272. The warrens are all out of use now, just as many of the thick woods of coppiced oak in the Moor edge valleys are no longer commercial. Once they were regularly cut and the bark went to the tanneries at Okehampton. Moretonhampstead. Tavistock and above all Plymouth. Nor is peat cut any more, though on the high northern Moor the deep trenches and signs of cutting are still visible. Apart from the roads, the arrivals of railways around the Moors in 1850–70 encouraged commercial ideas, and a railway was even built in 1879 from Bridestowe station 5 miles into the Moor to Rattlebrook Head to develop the peat beds there. The railway has gone, and none of the ideas for using the peat lasted long. Only one passenger railway ran into the Moor proper, the Yelverton-Princetown line which followed the route of Tyrwhitt's tramway and was working from 1883 until 1956.

Rivalling Tyrwhitt in the south-eastern corner of the Moor was George Templer, who built a horse-drawn tramway, the trucks running not on rails but granite sets, up to the quarries at Haytor. It was in operation from 1820 to 1858 and the quarry did provide granite for the London Bridge of 1825 which was shipped to Arizona in 1970. There were quarries all round the Moor and the granite for Nelson's Column came from Foggin Tor, but today only the Merrivale quarry is in operation.

The quarries needed explosives and Powder Mills Farm, half way between Postbridge and Two Bridges and just north of the road, still has the ruins of a gunpowder factory and its chimney stacks. The mortar which was used to test the powder was taken by American troops in Word War II, but they were persuaded to return it.

The one flourishing industry today is the winning of china clay at Lee Moor and Wotter, in the south-west corner. Certain granites decompose – growan, the moormen call the soft rock – and in its final state of decay the felspar yields china clay, used not only in pottery but paper-making and a vast range of products. It has a high export value, but, because for every ton of clay won there are 8 tons of waste, Lee Moor not only has vast pits – the largest extends over a hundred acres and is over 300ft deep – but accompanying waste heaps which can be seen even well out in the English Channel. Expansion plans will divert the Cadover-Cornwood road and make a pit 2½ miles long and 1½ miles across.

The area is dramatic, dusty and frightening in its scale, but its impact could be reduced by using the waste instead of tearing up the Home Counties with gravel pits, and by a much greater respect for the amenities of the countryside.

Army training grounds

Another disfiguring activity is the use of the Moor by the services for training. The military first came in 1873 and two years later set up a camp above Okehampton. Over the years they expanded, firing artillery, mortars and small arms in field exercises. By the end of World War II they had spread over almost all Dartmoor and, after violent local protests, announced that they wanted to keep 72,000 acres, with the public permanently excluded from 52,000. A deal was made with Devon County Council which eventually reduced their total training areas to just under 50,000 acres, mostly north of the Moretonhampstead-Tavistock road. Since the designation of Dartmoor as a National Park in 1951 and a fatal accident in 1958 there have been minor reductions and concessions. But whether soldiers derive any benefit from rehearsing the Boer War in this age, or their use of a National Park for firing shells and bombs, is hotly debated. Military occupation has been established on the crest of the Moor above Okehampton, and driven a metalled road deep into the wildest part of the northern quarter.

Reservoirs have also reached the Moor to water the growing towns. Burrator (completed 1898) and Fernworthy (1942), with their encircling plantations, are attractive places because the approach roads enable visitors to look down on the water, whereas in the Avon valley (1954) and at Meldon (1970) the dams are first seen as ugly walls across the valleys. Those who knew these valleys before they were flooded realise that even Burrator must have been as beautiful before the dam as it is now.

The other modern intrusion, largely between the wars, has been the planting of thousands of acres with softwoods, mainly Sitka spruce, by the Forestry Commission. These blanket plantings have changed the character of the Moor and denied large areas to walkers.

Undoubtedly Dartmoor's main value to the nation in modern times is as a place for open air recreation, for walking and exploring one of the few wilderness areas left in England, and certainly the only one in the whole of the south. Dartmoor was made a National Park in 1951, but this did not make it national property. The Forest is still owned by the Duchy of Cornwall and the surrounding areas, however wild they may look, are privately owned. Even the commons have their owners and the common rights are limited to other property owners, though under the Dartmoor Commons Act of 1985 access on foot and horseback has been legalised. Designation as a National Park merely gives a higher degree of planning control; it is a place where first the natural amenities and second the need of people for open-air recreation, must be considered in all developments. But people still live and work on Dartmoor and their rights and their farms must be protected; without them indeed the Moor would be a sorry place. Even so motorists and walkers who behave sensibly, and have some understanding of the Moor, are most welcome.

A sun burst through heavy cloud outlines the dramatic shape of a walker on one of Hound Tor's many rocky outcrops.

Weather and Wildlife

Dartmoor bears the full brunt of the rain-bearing south-westerly winds sweeping in from the Atlantic, so it is naturally wetter, windier and, because of its height, less mild than the rest of Devon. 'Nine months winter and three months spring' is how Princetown people describe their weather, but they are on the wettest, most exposed side of the Moor. While the average rainfall for the whole Moor is 62in, Fernworthy's average is 34in and Princetown rejoices in 82in. Quite often it records over 100 inches a year, and its highest figure was 115 inches for 1882. Yet its mean annual temperature is only 4°F lower than Torquay, and the daily average of sunshine little lower. There are days when the Moor is swathed in low cloud and the coast is clear, and other days when Dartmoor is in bright sun and sea mists shroud the coastal areas. While lowland Devon only has snow lying for an average of 5 days a year, Dartmoor's figure is 15–20 with over 30 days on the highest ground. At intervals a particularly bad winter buries the Moor under snow for weeks on end and isolates villages and lonely farms.

Woodlands range from the deep combes where the rivers cut their way out of the Moor, mainly inhabited by oak, through the regimented plantations of modern forestry to the three survivals of the primaeval forest on the high Moor. There is Black Tor Beare in the West Okement valley, above Meldon Reservoir; Pile's Copse on the Erme above Harford; and, best known of all, Wistman's Wood on the West Dart above Two Bridges. The trees, again mainly oak, are estimated to be between 300 and 500 years old.

The open Moor again varies, basically between wet and dry moor (though even the 'dry' moor can give wet feet in many seasons). On the high watersheds of both northern and southern moors are large blanket bogs. The northern bog stretches for many miles and the peat is broken by black gullies in places 6 feet deep which leave the walker jumping from hag to hag. The southern bog is smaller, the peat less deep, and not broken by gullies. With a few exceptions most major Devon rivers rise in these two bogs, though it is hard when tracing the head of a river to tell where bog ends and river starts. The rivers create more bogs as they come down from the heights; at the various old sea levels where wide valleys were formed and the river slows there is often a flat basin where the vegetation seems like a mat floating on a lake, and if you venture into it the ground for several feet around quakes and undulates. Just to increase the problems of the walker, there are even hillside bogs where the tributary streams coming into the valleys fill hollows, from which the rock has eroded, with silt and bog. Clumps of reed, cotton grass with their telltale white tufts, bright green sphagnum moss, purple moor grass and some heathers clothe the boggy areas.

On the 'dry' moor the vegetation is grass, heather, gorse, whortleberries in places and, on the lower levels, bracken. To produce more food for their animals the moormen regularly burn or 'swale' the heather in spring; where this has been overdone the heather is weakened, and this may be one reason for the great spread of bracken in recent decades. The gorse can be circled or animal paths followed through it.

Lark song and buzzard cry

Away from the wooded and pastoral edges, where the birds and mammals can find food and shelter, the Moor can be strangely silent. Buzzards, carrion crows and ravens range the open ground for food, kestrels nest on some of the tors, and the commonest breeding birds are meadow pipits and skylarks. For many the song of a spiralling lark and the mew of a gliding buzzard are the most evocative sounds of Dartmoor. Stonechats and winchats like the gorse, wheatears nest in the walls and wrens frequent the rocky gulleys.

As one gets higher, nearer the central bogs, so the bird life becomes thinner. Snipe and the common sandpiper can be found there, and in summer the curlew. When they move off to the estuaries in winter large flocks of starlings – 'them there Russian birds' as one old Dartmoor man calls them – arrive. A huge flock will nearly destroy a wood which it takes over, but the wheeling masses coming in to roost of a winter's evening can be most dramatic. Game birds are rare, but the reservoirs are bringing wildfowl to the Moor and the Forestry Commission plantations have increased the number of breeding species of birds.

Rabbits were common before myxomatosis nearly wiped them out, but colonies do crop up and flourish in various areas before the disease comes in again. They also have enemies in the many foxes on the Moor; apart from the rabbit these are the most likely mammals to be seen although their natural cunning and good camouflage does not make spotting them easy. The Moor has no deer, and few hares. Badgers may range the open ground for food but their setts, with a few exceptions, are close to the in-country woodlands. Otters live by the streams, but, like the badgers, one rarely sees them.

There are stoats and weasels, but the smaller mammals are mainly to be found in the woodlands which also afford rich hunting ground for insect life. There is a large bat population. Lizards and adders are common; grass snakes rather less so, but nearly always the adder will hear the walker and be off before it is even seen.

Storm clouds over the Northern Moor.

The Motorist's Moor

One essential: the map

An essential piece of equipment is the Ordnance Survey 1-inch Tourist Map of Dartmoor. It covers all the Moor and includes Exeter, Torbay and Plymouth. The relief colouring gives an instant view of the whole territory and colour hatching emphasises the lie of the land. Green woodlands, blue rivers and reservoirs, the conventional signs for marsh and rock – all build up the natural picture. The major antiquities are marked as well as the viewpoints – which even tell you which way to look – and the danger areas of the military firing ranges. The actual boundaries of the ranges are not marked but if you are approaching an area where the map is marked 'danger area' in red, watch for the red flags.

The best guide of all is the colour coded signposts, unique to Dartmoor. The best roads, for the most relaxing drive, suitable for most vehicles, have black-edged signs. Blue-edged signs suit medium vehicles, brown-edged signs are really only suitable for cars, while the traditional white signposts are most difficult, often only giving access to a small hamlet or a single farm. In addition the Park Authority also publishes a most useful leaflet, 'What to See from Dartmoor's Main Roads'.

It has always been the policy of the National Park Committee to encourage caravan sites round the edge of the Moor. They were instrumental, for example, in establishing a very pleasant site among trees on the banks of the Dart at Buckfast. But from what has been said about the roads it must be clear that Dartmoor proper is not caravan country; a Moor-edge base is happier both for caravanners and the other drivers on the road.

Accommodation

Motorists seeking a base for a Dartmoor holiday have a wide choice. There are three large urban areas, with wide ranges of hotel accommodation, shops, cinemas, restaurants and the like, in the cathedral city of Exeter (45 minutes to the open Moor), the seaside resorts of Torbay (30–45 minutes) and the largest of all, the historic seaport of Plymouth (20 minutes). Then there are the market towns round the Moor: Ashburton, Buckfastleigh, Tavistock and Okehampton, and rather smaller places like Moretonhampstead, South Brent, Ivybridge and Lydford. At heart they are all working towns, service and shopping centres for their neighbourhoods, but as tourism increases its hold on South Devon so these places cater more, and more ably, for the visitors. The two small towns most developed in this respect, however, are Chagford, which has a century's experience of cater-

ing for visitors and was the original base of Dartmoor visitors; and Bovey Tracey, whose hotels and shops have developed because of its position on the tourist route from Torquay to the Moor. But outside the true urban areas there are small towns, ranging in population from 7,000 down to 1,500, down to large village standards.

There is in fact ample accommodation on and around Dartmoor. The English Tourist Board publishes a list of over two hundred places offering at least bed and breakfast, and another list almost as long of self-catering accommodation. Both are available in ample detail from the Dartmoor National Park Authority. In addition the Dartmoor Tourist Association produces an attractive booklet listing not only accommodation available from their members but other attractions and lists of places to see. Another useful booklet is the Dartmoor and South Devon Farm and Country Holidays which has maps, a drawing of each establishment and a general account of what is on offer.

Dartmoor's only four star hotel, also isolated but in a park rather than on the Moor, is the Manor House Hotel, Moretonhampstead. It was the manor house of North Bovey, rebuilt with nineteenth-century opulence by the original W. H. Smith, and turned by the old Great Western Railway into Devon's answer to Gleneagles.

Dartmoor normally has room for everyone, but it must be remembered that if the place you first try is full, the next may be some miles off. So start looking early for the unbooked bed.

Roads around the Moor

Some motorists may just see Dartmoor in passing, as they travel from England to Cornwall. For the best views they will take the southerly Plymouth route going west, and come back on the A30 through Okehampton, north of the Moor. The motorway from Bristol (M5) or the A30 or A303 from London all lead to the Exeter bypass and the A38 to Plymouth. The Exeter-Plymouth road now is dual carriageway all the way, and built motorway style though it only has two lanes in each direction. There is a long climb to the ridge of Haldon but on the run down the whole eastern skyline of Dartmoor opens out, from the rounded curve of Cawsand Hill at the northern end through the dominant Haytor Rocks, which at times seem directly ahead. Soon after the Ashburton exits the Dart itself is crossed at Buckfast and then the road curls round the southern buttresses of Brent Hill and Western Beacon close on the right hand. From the roundabout at Marsh Mills where you cross the Plym and can see still on the right the china clay hills of Lee Moor, Plymouth can be avoided by taking the second exit to the Tamar Bridge (toll) and Saltash.

After Sourton Cross – where the Tavistock road joins from the right – the Okehampton bypass is now being built. What it will do to this edge of the

National Park remains to be seen, but at the time of writing the old road still drops down to Okehampton with the Moor still dramatic on the right and the last run down through Okehampton Park a well-wooded stretch. If the trees are bare Okehampton Castle itself, from which the first Norman earls of Devon dominated the county, can be seen also on the right. After Okehampton the road winds round the northern end of the Moor to Sticklepath, with its rescued water mill driving so many tools, and Ramsley. This road is the northern boundary of the National Park from Sourton Cross to Cheriton Bishop, but the quality of this north-eastern corner is in the Teign valley, and not to be seen from the road.

None of these routes so far have crossed open moorland, which most of all gives motorists the Dartmoor feeling. The only one of the roads round the Moor which does this is A386, which leaves A30 a few miles west of Okehampton and goes through Tavistock to Plymouth. The westbound motorist might on another variation follow A30 from Exeter through Okehampton to Sourton Cross and then take A386 south to the Tamar Bridge. Apart from the drab open stretch of Prewley Moor the drive is between stone hedges until Lydford is passed, but the road sits tight under the western scarp of the Moor with a splendid skyline on the left. If you park on the open moor immediately past Lydford the town itself and its castle, the tinners' gaol, can be seen to the west as well as the line of Lydford Gorge, where the river Lyd has carved its most dramatic exit from the high Moor.

The A386 climbs on across Black Down and the shoulder of Gibbet Hill, still with the main mass of the Moor on the left hand and the volcanic peak of Brent Tor, capped by its church, to the south-west.

Plymouth Road runs out between villas built out of nineteenth-century mining profits to a statue of Sir Francis Drake, who was born nearby at Crowndale, and then climbs out of the Tavy valley to drop down through woods to Magpie Bridge on the Walkham. Then a long climb takes the road to Yelverton and 3 miles of open country across Roborough Down.

A timeless view: a country lane near Goodameavy.

The Walker's Moor

The only way to know Dartmoor, to get the real feel of the wilderness, to enjoy its solitude, is to walk it. There is really no other way because the roads certainly do not get to the best places, whether in the sheltered wooded valleys or the high wilderness. There are regular bus routes encircling the Moor, Exeter-Okehampton-Tavistock-Yelverton-Plymouth, and Plymouth-Ivybridge-Buckfastleigh-Ashburton-Chudleigh-Exeter, and in summertime the splendid Transmoor Link, service no 82, which links Plymouth and Exeter right across the centre of the Moor by double-decker bus. But since the privatisation of bus services things are much in the melting pot, generally much improved, and a number of smaller companies are now running their own routes.

For the main routes it is worth getting the Western National timetable from their office in Queen Street, Exeter for a few pence. There are also weekly 'travel anywhere' tickets, and leaflets suggesting walks linked with bus services, available from their office. Western National at Laira Bridge, Plymouth, also have a useful timetable of their services to the western edge of the Moor, and Plymouth Citybus from their offices at Milehouse, Plymouth, also publish a timetable covering Shaugh and Bickleigh as well. If one is concerned with the smaller villages, and many of them have bus links even if it is only on one or two days a week, it is as well to write to the Dartmoor National Park office at Parke, Bovey Tracey, indicating the area of interest. The old 'Pony Express' service has been replaced by the Dartmoor Hoppa and does reach out into odd corners, even nearly to the head of Burrator on Sundays.

A walk on the moor is a laudable intention, but it will be much more rewarding if you have a particular goal, such as climbing a tor.

The map

For many walks the 1-inch Tourist Ordnance Survey map is good enough, but it has limitations; you can for instance climb a tor with its aid because a tor is not hard to find. But look for a group of hut circles marked on the 1-inch map, particularly in a good clitter area, and that is another matter. Ideally for elusive targets one needs the 6-inch map, but they are awkward to carry and cover little ground. The 2½-inch Ordnance Survey maps are far more satisfactory: the 1:25,000 series. The old First and Second series have now been replaced by the Outdoor Leisure series in which No 28 covers all Dartmoor in colour and marks the rights of way.

The compass

Now the finest map in the world is not a lot of use without a compass to which it can be orientated; how good or what kind of compass is up to the experience of its user. Dartmoor in places can present a featureless face and a thoroughly familiar tor can look quite different seen from the other side.

You must also be able to walk to a compass bearing. With the instrument's aid identify two or more objects on your route – a tree, a tor, anything – and then walk towards it. Have two or three because the roll of the ground can mean that the tor chosen as the next objective can disappear after two minutes' walking. In fact anyone not experienced in wilderness walking will be wise to make the first venture with someone who is. That is not difficult nowadays because the Dartmoor National Park Committee has been organising guided walks all over the Moor since 1974. Several hundred are planned each year from about a dozen starting points, varying from family walkabouts of an hour and a half duration to six hour jobs. Different walks cover different points of interest; mines, natural history, archaeology; some have a mix of interests. The starting points are well-marked, from car parks often with lavatories. Guides have arm-bands as identification. In 1985 some four thousand people enjoyed these walks, averaging on each between nine and fifteen people so that one is not in too large a party. Leaflets can be obtained from the National Park office giving details.

There are also available from the National Park office a series of four booklets giving detailed walks with clear directions and much information, as well as a 'Bus-away-Walk-a-day' booklet which explains itself.

Pace yourself sensibly

We all believe we can walk 4 miles an hour though not many of us really can, even on roads, and if you are walking for a long period it is wise to allow 10 minutes' rest in each hour. But there is no real point in going to Dartmoor to walk on roads; that can be done anywhere in Britain, and the whole merit of Dartmoor is that it is wilderness, you can take off into open country, get away from roads. So get off the roads, but remember that you do not travel so fast on rough ground, that an uphill stretch can be a lot further than the map (which after all is only a flat picture) suggests, that there may be a lot to stop and study, and the steeper the hill the more often you need to draw breath.

Allow for changing weather

Plan in advance; like choosing a holiday, the anticipation can be as pleasant as the achievement. But plans are only plans, not compulsory exercises; *check the weather* before the start. The most up-to-date can be obtained by

Devonport Leat originally carried water from the West Dart and Cowsic Rivers to the town of Devonport. It has since been diverted to help supply Burrator Reservoir. Here it winds around a hillside near Nun's Cross Farm, having just emerged from a tunnel.

telephoning Plymouth (0752) 8091. These weather reports come from RAF Mount Batten meteorological office, which is admirably situated just south-west of the Moor – but it is at sea level and, as local people will tell you, the south coast of Devon is a different world to Dartmoor. If you want to be absolutely sure telephone Plymouth 42534, which is the Mount Batten exchange, and ask for the Met Office; tell them whereabouts you plan to walk on the Moor and they can be much more precise.

Remember that the weather can change fast, and the best weathermen can only forecast, not give a guarantee. Hot summer days can bring their own fog, winter rain can turn to sleet or snow, fresh winds can get stronger and be merciless on high ground. So always plan your route with two thoughts: your objective and your escape route. If it is a fine sunny day with an improving weather outlook then make that epic strike out, and just be aware that if mist should arise then there is a track or a river not so far away that will lead back to civilisation without plunging you through too many bogs. If there is wind and rain about, then have in mind a return route in the lee of higher ground which will give some shelter. Remember that there is all the difference in wind and rain behind you or in your face: if you do go out in those conditions head out into the weather so that you will not push too far, and will have the weather behind you on the home-ward stretch. It may be true that wind blows away fog, but often on the Moor you can be caught in low cloud on a windy day, and that swirling blustering wetness can be thoroughly unpleasant. Even so there can be an exhilaration and a challenge in such weather; just do not be foolhardy.

Clothing is important. Warm, comfortable, wind and water proof are the basic requirements. Better too many clothes than not enough, but a small rucksack is handy if you want to shed sweaters. Old clothes that will not suffer from a little black mud are best. Keeping out wind and rain is vital, for failure to do so can be fatal. Wind and wet produce a lowering of the body temperature which in turn speeds exhaustion, a very quick killer. Heavy oldfashioned mackintoshes not only let the rain through eventually but they also get heavy with the wetness. There is one experienced walker who for years never used more than an ordinary plastic mackintosh but he is old and wily about his escape routes, and even he is now to be seen in a light plastic anorak and trousers. The anorak by itself is not enough; the legs need protection from wind, rain and the water running off an anorak. Warm old trousers and warm jerseys are still needed under these covers, if they are thin.

Footwear is a matter of choice. It is not very wise to wear big boots if the feet are unaccustomed to them, but good ankle boots are probably best. Ideally they should be big enough to fit snugly over ordinary woollen socks and a second pair of short thick woollen socks which can be turned down around the ankles as a cushion against the boots. Many walkers prefer thick rubber soles, serrated to give a good grip, to the hob-nailed soles of some hill walkers, because they find nails slip on rock.

Sense and safety

All of which sounds desperately alarming, as if the Dartmoor venturer takes his life in his hands. In reality it is safer than motoring. Bad weather on the Moor can kill, but you challenge the weather according to your experience; the aim is to enjoy the place and not indulge in self-punish-ment. Fog and bog are the traditional enemies, and the ways of coping with both are soon learned.

Use your escape route if you see visibility closing in, if there is any advance sign; do not wait for it to happen. If visibility is really too bad for normal navigation go downhill, and keep downhill, till a stream is found and follow that down. Sooner or later it will reach habitation or a road, but if you have worked out that escape route you will know where it takes you. If it does lead you into boggy land then very often the actual bed of the stream is the firmest ground, and your feet will be no wetter than strug-gling in the marsh.

As the geological chapter explained, you can expect marshy conditions on high ground, watersheds where the rain has not made up its mind which way to flow. These are marked on the map, and will be wetter after a period of rain than after drought. In fact the driest time in these areas is in a hard frost, but usually bogs just have to be suffered. The tufts of reeds and moor grass afford the best support. Then in all valleys, and at varying heights, are the basins, often quite wide, where the river is sluggish and the flat surface a real bog. The best known is Fox Tor Mires, south of Princetown. These areas can be recognised by their vegetation, tufts of marsh grass and reeds and in summer the white plumes of the marsh cotton. Your feet will soon tell you if you miss these signs, and the real bogs will frighten you off with the whole surface of the ground rippling for several yards around with each movement of your feet. But you should see them coming, and they can be avoided by keeping to the higher ground round the edge. Almost certainly the stream will come down a steeper gradient to the mire and leave it by a small cleave with obviously steeper sides. As a rule it is easier to cross the river here than above the mire, but the choice depends on your route. Good hill walkers never give away altitude; every time you go down a few feet you will have to climb up again, and it is often less tiring to walk a little further and keep your height.

The third kind of bog, the 'featherbeds' on the hillsides which are often unpleasantly deep pits of water covered with vegetation, usually mark themselves with bright green grass. They are small and easy to circle round. Indeed always go round bogs and mires; it may look quicker to go straight on but the crossing will be much more tiring than walking a little

The low winter sun makes interesting
shadow patterns in this Northern Moor
landscape.

further, and many can be dangerous. You will soon learn to recognise the signs, and the rule always is common sense.

Apart from bogs there are rivers. The nearer the source the narrower and shallower they are, of course, but most are shallow in places and so studded with boulders that it is possible to cross without difficulty, though you may have to range up or downstream a little to find convenient rocks. These rivers are the fastest to rise after heavy rain of any in England, and in spate they can be killers. The unwise have been swept away by the force of water and the Dart has a folklore reputation of claiming a heart every year. But when they are dangerous they look dangerous. Do not then be foolhardy; it is better to follow a river down until a bridge is found, or to change your plans altogether if a river looks threatening.

Regulate clothing and footwear to your intentions, but be sensible if you are going far. Take maps and a compass, and a torch if there is any likelihood of being overtaken by darkness. At night every stone and tuft of heather is a stumbling block. Youngsters nowadays are taught to take a whistle too, in case they get lost, or fall. They are never sent out on Duke of Edinburgh expeditions in parties of less than five so that if one is hurt, two can stay and the others go for help.

If you are going deep into the Moor, tell someone where you are going, and when you will be back. Tell them when you get back. If there is no one to tell, put a note under the windscreen wiper of your car. Failing all else, tell the nearest police station. There is a Dartmoor rescue organisation, efficient and well-equipped, which can find people if they know where to start looking, but no one wants to have them called out, any more than a yachtsman wants to fire red flares for the lifeboat.

Having looked after yourself, you must also look after Dartmoor. There are 365 square miles in the National Park but every inch of it is private property and should be treated as such. Of that area about a half is enclosed farmland, which must be respected like all farmland. Keep out of the fields, unless the map or signpost shows a right of way, and even then keep to the path and shut the gates. On either side of the cross roads in the centre of the Moor are the large enclosures. They are mainly used for grazing and some owners do not object to sensible walkers. Often between the enclosures are drift lanes which enabled cattle to be brought off the Moor; use them if you are in these areas. Do not climb the stone walls; the stones resist the weather but not scramblers. If by mischance you do dislodge stones, replace them. Hedges and stone walls are marked on the 2½in maps. Excluding the afforested areas there are about 120,000 acres of open country, which should be enough. Of these the military use some 32,000 acres for training.

On the open Moor you are still on private property. Commoners have grazing rights here by law; the rest of us have a right of long custom rather than of law. So the Country Code is scrupulously observed: no litter above all. Dogs must be kept under control. Keep away from grazing stock. The ponies and the cattle, even the wildest Scottish beasts, are not likely to harm you but they are not used to people, and the wilder the country the less familiar the livestock is with humanity. Even ponies which haunt the roadsides can kick out and break adult ribs. In the lambing season ewes will sometimes graze a long way from their offspring; do not let a bleating lonely lamb excite your sentimentality. It is not lost, does not want picking up and carrying to the nearest ewe or farm. Experienced Moor walkers in their time have put a sheep on its back over on its legs, or cut free from some heavily-fleeced animal tangled in brambles. But as a basic rule keep away from the animals. Their survival rate is better than ours in the main, and if in doubt go to the nearest habitation.

Some may want to make a walk of several days, bivouacking on the Moor. If there is a house or farm in sight, go and ask for a site. If it is quite wild country, no one is likely to object to a one-night stand if the usual proprieties of camping are observed.

If a base camp of several days is planned, then permission must be sought. The sensible thing anyway then is to seek out a farmer and ask for a site not too far from the farm. Most of the moormen are reasonable people and may even be glad of a fresh face and a talk. But they do not welcome fools, and no one should plan any kind of camp on Dartmoor without experience in the business.

Whiteworks cottages, on the edge of old mine workings near Princetown.

The Wooded Valleys

The 'beauty spots' of Dartmoor in the Victorian sense were all in the steep-sided valleys where the rivers carve their ways out of the Moor proper down to the pastoral in-country. Gothic woods of ancient gnarled oaks shade mossy dells on the banks of splashing clear rivers, gurgling over mossy rocks to waterfalls edged by luxuriant ferns. Anathema to the modern forester but a paradise for the botanist, these corners are still pretty where they have survived. But the Victorians were nurtured not only in romantic dells but in the belief that walking was good for the mind as well as the body, spiritually uplifted by the exercise required to get to these places and poetically moved when they arrived. In our century many of these places – Lydford Gorge, Bickleigh Vale, Hawns and Dendles, Lustleigh Cleave, Becky Falls, Fingle Bridge – have gone from the tourist routes because they do entail walking. But locals still know and cherish them.

To understand these valley woodlands it might be best first of all to go to Yarner Wood, near Bovey Tracey, on the road to Becky Falls and Manaton. This is a National Nature Reserve and the Nature Conservancy Council have now established two trails through the woods. The entrance is at the bottom of Reddaford Water hill, booklets are available to explain the ecological background and there are explanatory exhibits beside the trails. The Nature Conservancy kept these woods closed for many years but now the old permit system has gone and visitors are welcome.

The geological tilt of the Moor means that the rivers on the northern and western sides are fewer, shorter and tend not to be wooded. The exception is Lydford Gorge, now National Trust property, the most dramatic of all and with all the Victorian qualities. It is only open 'in the season' but even then after rain the rocky path can be slippery and the handrails, in some places on goat tracks hanging over swirling waters, are minimal. There is a car park beside the bridge just south of Lydford village: do not be frightened by the view over the parapet of the bridge into the green depths or by the initial snaking path down into the gloom. You can almost see the river cutting down into the rock, the whirlpools still polishing the smooth-sided rock basins. The bridge end is most dramatic and after a while the river's urgency eases as it flows through gentler wooded dells. A high waterfall adds a last touch of drama and a pub is conveniently outside the bottom gate. The car however is 2 miles back up a not-very-exciting road, and while in past summers a pony and trap plied for hire along this road it is more fun to walk back through the gorge than along the road.

The Plym has all the qualities of the southern rivers and Bickleigh Vale was its great attraction. The southern end, from Plym Bridge, is still popular and the right bank is another National Trust property. Plym Bridge was first mentioned in 1238 and in 1450 was a place of pilgrimage because 'of the many miracles which God has wrought' in a chapel on the bridge. Just east of the bridge is a wooden viaduct, survival of an incline on the china clay tramway from Plymouth to Lee Moor; the full trucks descending hauled up the empty trucks. The entrance to Bickleigh Vale is on the right of the road to Roborough and a woodland path follows the river to a point opposite. Cann Quarry, for centuries the main source of slates for the area but now a haunt of ravens. The disused Great Western Railway line to Tavistock runs through the valley with several high viaducts; apart from the meadows beside the Plym at Riverford, it is a woodland walk for most of the way to Bickleigh Bridge. The old trees have been left in the bottom but most of the slopes now are Forestry Commission softwoods. While the lower stretch of the Vale is firm walking the top is little used and can get very muddy; otherwise it is still one of the best woodland walks.

Nowadays more people go to Shaugh Bridge, a couple of miles above Bickleigh Bridge and at the confluence of the Plym and its tributary the Meavy. Between them rises the craggy Dewerstone, its slopes covered with old coppice oaks. The immediate area is trampled down to bare rock and earth by over-use but the setting is still magnificent and a scramble up either river bank a delight. The Plym is milky with china clay from the Cadover area but the Meavy is limpid-clear. As well as the river walks you can climb up through the woods to the summit of Dewerstone and its tremendous views over Plymouth Sound.

An easier, less used and more varied route to the top is from Gooda-meavy Bridge, higher up the Meavy. Goodameavy can be reached from Shaugh Bridge by following the road sign-posted to Yelverton, or by leaving the Plymouth–Yelverton road on Roborough Down by the Clearbrook turning, and taking the right fork after the road crosses the Plymouth leat (which Sir Francis Drake built in 1590–1). At Goodameavy there is a stile with a National Trust sign on the east side of the river and the path, through fields at first, follows the line of a mineral railway built to serve a Dewerstone quarry. The path climbs gently through woods while the river drops away to the right. A blacksmith's cottage is now a Scout adventure training centre. At the end of the path you are halfway up the Dewerstone, but an inclined plane takes you higher and a final scramble reaches the summit. One of the rocks has several names carved on it; the notable one is Carrington, memorial to a Devonport schoolmaster devoted to the spot whose 2,000-line descriptive poem *Dartmoor* was first published in 1826. North-east of the summit are rocks which have a sheer face to the Plym. Wigford Down which stretches back from the Dewer-

The fern covered chasm of Lydford Gorge.

stone makes pleasant upland walking. North-east you can reach Cadover, north-west the moor gate by Urgles Farm and the steep lane back to Goodameavy. There is a medieval cross at the end of either of these walks.

Even more popular nowadays than Shaugh Bridge is Burrator, in the Meavy valley. Plymouth City bus line in summer extents the Dousland bus service nearly to the head of this reservoir, which serves the city and takes water from the source Drake used for his 1590 leat. It can be reached by road through Yelverton and Dousland and a road makes a complete circuit.

The Avon is less wooded but you can use the lane from South Brent past Lydia Bridge and through the hamlet of Lutton, and then the right of way to the disused sanatorium at Didworthy and on to Shipley Bridge. Higher up the valley is the Avon Dam and the water authority have gated the road beside the stream from Shipley Bridge up. It is still a good walking route to the open Moor, with the trees giving way to moorland vegetation, but the Avon Dam sits across it now like a forbidding wall.

The Dart valley

As one might expect, the Dart, greatest of all the Dartmoor rivers, also has some of the biggest woods and best gorges; the rich men of earlier years saw this too, and much of the best is hidden away in private parkland. But the National Trust has acquired land in the valley, notably a large area of woodland round Hembury Castle, on the right bank of the Dart north of Buckfast. Hembury (not to be confused with the greater 'castle' of the same date in east Devon) is typical of the early Iron Age defended sites of the Celts round the Moor, possibly protecting these new invaders from the older Bronze Age settlements on the Moor proper. The National Trust office at Saltram, near Plymouth, can supply a leaflet about the trail which they have laid out through these woods. The Trust also own the woods on the right bank of the Dart above New Bridge, and by crossing the bridge from the parking area a right of way can be found on the right which follows the river for some way and then climbs up the hill to Holne village.

There is also a stretch that can be explored downstream from New Bridge, where the minor road to Buckland-in-the-Moor follows the river for a mile before climbing steeply up through the woods to Buckland. Buckland Beacon has one of the best views on the Moor, and the village and church are worth exploring. Alternatively you can turn left-handed away from the Dart just before the confluence of the Webburn and take a minor road to Blackadon Tor and round to Poundsgate. The Dart valley is wooded for several miles above New Bridge and there is a scenic walk from the top of the hill leading to Poundsgate along Dr Blackall's grassed-over carriage drive that curves under Aish Tor and then northwards high above the river.

In the valley of the Bovey, above Bovey Tracey, Lustleigh Cleave is justly renowned. In many wooded valleys the trees hem in the visitor and limit his views but one side of the Cleave is open moorland, rising to impressive rock formations like the Nutcracker, a rocking or logan stone.

Raven's Tor and Fox's Yard in J. W. L. Page's 1892 *Exploration of Dartmoor* are described as 'ivy-mantled crag' and 'crannied pile'. Private enterprise foresters have been at work at the lower end of the valley, but either from Lustleigh or Manaton one can explore the Cleave. The area is criss-crossed with rights of way and a variety of bridges over the Bovey. The tors here barely top the thousand feet contour but they still have drama. The valleys face south-east and are warmer, less wet, more sheltered than much of the Moor, and the villages rich with thatch and luxuriant gardens. South of Manaton on a tributary of the Bovey, the Becka Brook, is Becky Falls.

The Teign valley from Newton Abbot north to Dunsford marks the division between Dartmoor and the Haldon ridge, and for much of its course is the eastern boundary of the National Park. From Chudleigh Bridge to Dunsford there is a pleasant B road and from Steps Bridge, just west of Dunsford on the Moretonhampstead road, stretches the longest of all the wooded valleys of the Moor, running nearly to Chagford. The river-side walk from Steps Bridge is renowned in spring for its wild daffodils and became so popular that now it is wardened in the key weeks to protect the flowers.

There has been much felling and conifer replanting in the Teign valley, but the next celebrated point is Fingle Bridge. One of the early achievements of the Dartmoor National Park was to persuade the owners of a tin teahut to replace it with a good building which the Park staff designed and which is now a good restaurant. It is little over a mile from the attractive little village of Drewsteignton but the roads to it are narrow and between high banks. Yet, as Crossing wrote in his classic *Guide to Dartmoor*, 'The Gorge of Fingle is the finest thing of its kind in the Westcountry'. The bridge is hardly wide enough for a single car; it was built for packhorses and only packhorse tracks wind away up the hill on the southern side. Probably it can be best appreciated by walking down the Fisherman's Path beside the river from Dogmarsh Bridge, near Sandypark, on the Bovey Tracey – Whiddon Down road near Chagford, and returning by the Hunter's Path, high above the river, by way of Sharp Tor and Hunter's Tor.

Winter sunshine filters through trees alongside the West Dart river near Dunnabridge.

The Moor North and South

Southern walks

For most of us the real joy of Dartmoor is to get away from the civilisation of our own day, out into the primeval Moor which has changed little over the centuries. It has been altered by man, of course; he has worshipped his prehistoric gods, built his farms, dug peat, mined tin. But in reality he has had little effect on the scene. 'Scratch my back,' says the old Dartmoor proverb, 'and I'll scratch your pocket.' And man has done little more than scratch the back of the wilderness. You can walk on springing turf under high skies into which the larks spiral, with the clear stream as company, and enjoy ever-changing views. Indeed the view can change so fast that even map-reading becomes a problem; that tor on which you fixed your gaze as your next mark disappears under a shoulder of hill as you advance; short-term and long-term landmarks are needed. So there is the sense of being in a private world (a rare enough pleasure these days), the comfort of the ranging hills, and the challenge of finding the way in strange country. Even tors look different from different angles.

To all this one can add the excitement of discovery, finding the traces of the man who passed this way before. It is not always easy. Vegetation can mask a stone row and a group of natural rocks can look like a stone circle.

The other merit of the open Moor is that you can plan any route to suit any day or any mood. Here are some suggestions:

Walk No 1: Princetown to Yelverton, 10 miles. *Mainly downhill, good going, long-range views. It can be shortened by using the bus from Burrator, Dousland or Meavy.*

Walk No 2: Cornwood to Ivybridge, 15 miles. *Fine views, source of rivers Yealm and Erme, edge of southern central fen, prehistory (the longest and the most prominent stone rows on Dartmoor), tin-mining and peat works.*

Walk No 3: Burrator to Childe's Tomb and back by Crazy Well Pool, 10 miles. *No great hill-climbing; prehistory, mining, a medieval legend and a major mire encircled.*

Walk No 4: Warren House Inn to Widecombe and either Bovey Tracey or Bickington, 12 miles. *High Moor, antiquities, mining, valley farms, fine tors and extensive views.*

The Northern Wilderness

The walker tackling Dartmoor north of the Tavistock-Two Bridges-Moretonhampstead road is going into the highest and wildest part of the Moor and will find two major restrictions: the military occupation and the central blanket bog, or fen. Of these the main deterrent is the military use, which entails field training with the firing of live ammunition from small arms, mortars and artillery on at least half the days in the year over a total area of about 30,000 acres. Another 4,665 acres are used in the south-western part of the Moor for 'dry' training, which means no live ammunition, and these areas are never closed.

In practice the northern area is divided into three separate ranges each with different sets of non-firing days. Their boundaries are marked by 7ft steel poles striped white and red, each visible from the next. Details are given in Appendix 1 together with a list of the places where the actual details are published, but as a basic guide the non-firing days are:

Merrivale. 8,742 acres stretching into the Moor from a southern boundary roughly parallel, and a mile or two north, of the road from Merrivale to Two Bridges, open every weekend, public holidays and all August.

Willsworthy. 3,447 acres east of Lydford, open weekends (except one a month), public holidays and all August.

Okehampton. 15,921 acres running south from the crest of the Moor above Okehampton, open every weekend, every summer evening, from 15 July to 15 September inclusive, a week at Easter and again at the Spring Bank Holiday, Christmas Day, Boxing Day and New Year's Day.

The ranges are marked with red flag which are flown from prominent tors all round the three ranges, and there are notice boards on the approaches warning people not to pass when the flags are flying. But the three ranges all meet on their interior boundaries and the fact that a walker finds no flags flying on one range does not mean necessarily that all the Moor is clear: you must watch for flags as you move from that free range towards another.

When in doubt, *keep out* is the safest advice. Weekly firing programmes are printed in three newspapers; post offices and pubs have maps of the ranges and firing dates, and you can also telephone for details. It pays to check in advance as well as to watch for flags; there has been one fatal accident to a walker since the last war.

The military occupation has also damaged the Moor physically with hutted camps at Okehampton and Willsworthy, a couple of rifle ranges at the latter place and, particularly in the Okehampton range, an extension and improvement of the old moormen's tracks. A metalled circuit in the north cuts into the deepest wilderness, and, to enable jeeps to take the red-flag-hoisters, tracks have been made to the top of various tors, including even Yes Tor and High Willhays. The walks suggested try to keep away from these disfigurements, and the Countryside Commission, the Dartmoor National Park Committee, the Dartmoor Preservation Association and other amenity bodies are constantly striving not only to reduce but to end the military occupation.

The central peat fen is a desolate area, and hard walking, but exhaustion is the main danger. Centuries ago the moormen cut a couple of 'passes' through the peat to enable cattle to be moved from north to south, or east to west, and an enthusiastic follower of hounds, Frank Phillpotts, made another nine in 1895–1905. Most of them were created by digging out the peat down to hard ground so that they appear as trenches. Some have been cleared and kept open by various people, including the Army, in modern times. They are mostly marked by memorial stones set up at each end by the two sons of Frank Phillpotts. On the 1-inch and metric Ordnance Survey map they are shown by black broken lines. They are listed with their map reference numbers in Appendix 2, and a map appears on page 124 but they are not always easy to find. Nor do they provide mud-free, hard walking ground, but they can help.

For over a century the mecca of walkers in the northern quarter has been Cranmere Pool. It is now no more than a black declivity in the heart of the fen and not even the source of a river, though the West Okement rises very near. But from its area the Taw and its streams rise to flow north, the Tavy west, the Teign east and the Dart south, so in many ways it can be seen as the heart of Devon. In 1854 James Perrott, the Chagford guide who could be called the father of Dartmoor walking, set up a cairn there and placed a bottle in the stones where visitors left their cards. Since then a letter box with its own 'Cranmere' stamp has been established, with a succession of visitors' books. The convention is to leave a postcard addressed to yourself in the box and sign the book, and to take any post-cards already in the box away for posting in an official postbox; so that you acquire proof of having reached Cranmere.

Because the military roads have made the pool easier of access in recent years, the hardier walkers no longer regard a Cranmere postcard as the ultimate accolade. Other letter boxes have been established, such as at Fur Tor a few miles south, and at Duck's Pool in the southern quarter, in the fen from which Plym, Avon, Erme and Swincombe rise. But Cranmere is still a magic word, and the four walks set out in this chapter can all be used to reach the letter box from the four sides of the northern quarter. In each case the final stretch to Cranmere can be hard going, especially after wet weather, once the central fen is met, and there is no disgrace in turning back short of the place. There are many hardy Moor walkers who have yet to reach Cranmere, and quite a few who have got close and then failed to find it. It is commonly agreed that Cranmere is best located from the northern side.

The cross of Childe's Tomb silhouetted dramatically against a stormy sky.

As a general rule the northern Moor is less rich in prehistory than the south, because then as now it was less hospitable to men. There is also less evidence of mining, though you can look for the ruined huts of the tinners, and the shelters of the peat cutters. Well out into the Moor the walker will still find enclosure walls, running across stretches of rough ground that look identical on either side, and ruined farmhouses, evidence of the greed of the enclosers and 'improvers' of the last century. They still serve as cattle enclosures and keep animals in bounds, and must not be damaged.

Walk No 5: Two Bridges, Wistman's Wood, Fur Tor letter box and returning to Two Bridges or Princetown. 15 miles, or with extension to Cranmere. 21 miles. *Good tors and views, some antiquities, the central fen. Some hard going.*

Walk No 6: Lydford to Tavy Cleave and Cranmere. 15 miles. *Dramatic scenery, some antiquities, the northern fen. Some hard going.*

Walk No 7: Chagford to Cranmere and back. 15 miles. *Lanes through farmland, antiquities, tors with good views, and a passage of the fen.*

Walk No 8: Okehampton by Meldon to High Willhays and Yes Tor, returning by the East Okement close to Belstone. 14 miles. Extension to Cranmere, another 4–5 miles. *Two contrasting river valleys, the highest points in southern England, wide-sweeping views, quarries, a reservoir dam and the artillery range.*

If from the main street of Okehampton you take the road up to the station a turning can be found on the right hand which leads into Okehampton Park. It soon turns into a footpath parallel to the West Okement river below.

All these walks in the northern Moor have reached Cranmere and obviously the various out and back routes could be linked by those with careful transport arrangements to cross the area from east to west, or north to south. But Cranmere is in the fen, and for many people it is hardly worth the effort. Each expedition gets the walker reasonably dry-shod to the edge of the fen and he may then be content to look and turn back. Most of the turning points are obvious and in themselves dramatic, and if there is any doubt about the weather, or the tiredness of the weakest member of the party, they should be the climax. None of this is easy country, and in each case the last lap, the final reach to Cranmere, is the hardest. No one should be led to believe that these are desperate, dangerous expeditions; they are for properly-dressed healthy people used to walking. Not even they should

be foolhardy, however, and the Dartmoor novice whose principal walk for fifty weeks of the year is to his garage or the bus stop should get some training – for his feet, his wind and his map-reading – on the lower slopes and the Moor edges.

Best of all, as has already been said but must be repeated, locate one of the guided tours conducted by the National Park authority and join it. The best way to learn about Moor walking, identifying landmarks, avoiding miry country, recognising the signs of the tin miners and the peat cutters, sorting the stone rows and the hut circles from the masses of clitter that can look man-arranged, is by going out with an expert. Everyone needs an apprenticeship and there are masters waiting. After that take to the Moor with confidence, map out your own routes, and perhaps one day you will join that select band who do not just have a Cranmere stamp on their belt, but have achieved the longest walk of all, Okehampton to Ivybridge in a day. There are not many who can claim that.

But the Moor is not for record breakers, or racers, or 'because it is there' characters. It is to be enjoyed, to be taken slowly, to be loved. Few people who have had the heather and the turf under their boots, the promised tor ahead, the clear stream at their side, the lark singing its heart out and the watching buzzard circling high above, ever get Dartmoor out of their minds again. In an increasingly hurrying noisy world it has the balm of peace.

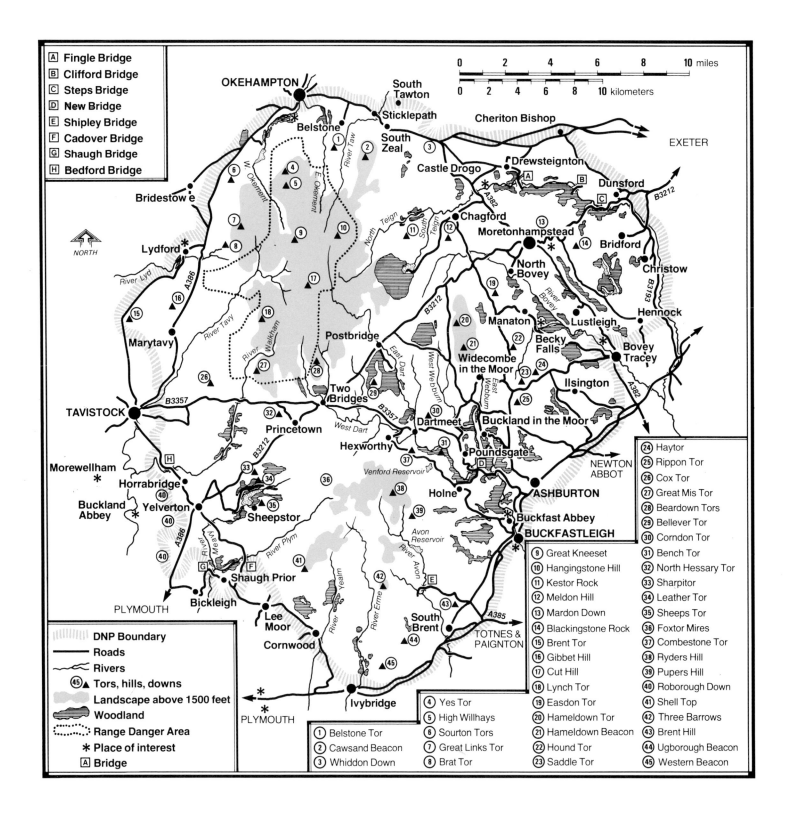

Legend (top left):

- A Fingle Bridge
- B Clifford Bridge
- C Steps Bridge
- D New Bridge
- E Shipley Bridge
- F Cadover Bridge
- G Shaugh Bridge
- H Bedford Bridge

Legend (bottom left):

- DNP Boundary
- Roads
- Rivers
- Tors, hills, downs
- Landscape above 1500 feet
- Woodland
- Range Danger Area
- * Place of interest
- A Bridge

Tors, hills, downs list:

1. Belstone Tor
2. Cawsand Beacon
3. Whiddon Down
4. Yes Tor
5. High Willhays
6. Sourton Tors
7. Great Links Tor
8. Brat Tor
9. Great Kneeset
10. Hangingstone Hill
11. Kestor Rock
12. Meldon Hill
13. Mardon Down
14. Blackingstone Rock
15. Brent Tor
16. Gibbet Hill
17. Cut Hill
18. Lynch Tor
19. Easdon Tor
20. Hameldown Tor
21. Hameldown Beacon
22. Hound Tor
23. Saddle Tor
24. Haytor
25. Rippon Tor
26. Cox Tor
27. Great Mis Tor
28. Beardown Tors
29. Bellever Tor
30. Corndon Tor
31. Bench Tor
32. North Hessary Tor
33. Sharpitor
34. Leather Tor
35. Sheeps Tor
36. Foxtor Mires
37. Combestone Tor
38. Ryders Hill
39. Pupers Hill
40. Roborough Down
41. Shell Top
42. Three Barrows
43. Brent Hill
44. Ugborough Beacon
45. Western Beacon

Map labels include: OKEHAMPTON, South Tawton, Sticklepath, Cheriton Bishop, EXETER, Belstone, South Zeal, Castle Drogo, Drewsteignton, Dunsford, Bridestowe, Chagford, Moretonhampstead, Bridford, Christow, Lydford, North Bovey, Hennock, Manaton, Lustleigh, Becky Falls, Bovey Tracey, Marytavy, Postbridge, Widecombe in the Moor, Ilsington, Two Bridges, Buckland in the Moor, TAVISTOCK, Princetown, Dartmeet, Hexworthy, Poundsgate, NEWTON ABBOT, Morewellham, Horrabridge, Buckland Abbey, Yelverton, Sheepstor, Venford Reservoir, Holne, ASHBURTON, Buckfast Abbey, BUCKFASTLEIGH, Avon Reservoir, PLYMOUTH, Bickleigh, Shaugh Prior, Lee Moor, Cornwood, South Brent, TOTNES & PAIGNTON, Ivybridge

Rivers labelled: River Taw, W. Okement, E. Okement, River Lyd, River Tavy, River Walkham, North Teign, South Teign, River Bovey, East Dart, West Webburn, East Webburn, West Dart, River Meavy, River Plym, River Yealm, River Erme, River Avon

Roads: A382, A386, B3212, B3357, B3193, A385

NORTH

Scale: 0–10 miles / 0–10 kilometers

29

Appendices

Appendix 1

A sketch map showing the Dartmoor firing ranges can be seen in local post offices, hotels, inns etc.

The Dartmoor Firing Notice is issued weekly to local post offices etc, and is also published on Fridays for the following week in *The Western Morning News*, the *Express and Echo*, Exeter, and the *Western Times*, Exeter. The firing dates can also be obtained by telephoning police stations and post offices near the ranges, or by using the telephone answering service on Torquay 24592, Exeter 70164, Plymouth 701924 and Okehampton 2939.

Appendix 2

A list of the peat passes, with six-figure map reference to Sheet SX of the National Grid, based on a paper published in the *Devonshire Association Transactions* for 1965, Vol XCVII, 'The Phillpotts peat passes of northern Dartmoor' by Brian Le Messurier.

Whitehorse Hill (619854–617854). 270yds. Memorial stones.

East Dart Head (614852–613851). 40yds. Memorial stones.

Marsh Hill (620826–617823). 350yds. Memorial stones.

Flat Tor (613814–612813). c 50yds. Memorial stones.

North-West Passage (603822–603823; 602824–598827). 450yds. Memorial stones and cairns.

Walkham Head (579815–578814). 150yds. Memorial stones.

Little Kneeset (592844–592841). 360yds. Memorial stones.

Black Ridge (597858–595849). 1,100yds. Memorial stones and small cairns.

Okement Hill (603869–601868). 230yds. Cairns.

Appendix 3

Letter Boxes

Postcards may be left at these boxes for the next visitor to post. Many boxes have a visitors' book and a rubber stamp and pad, but the stamp should not be used to frank the postage stamp though it may be impressed on another part of the card. Some boxes are in the firing areas, and some are of a temporary nature which come and go. In recent years a mass of new boxes have been established and hunts for them have almost become a craze, so much so that while a new breed of Dartmoor walkers has been established some have become careless of the Moor, tearing up turf and dislodging stones in their searches for some elusive boxes. Even a number of pubs and hotels now have their own visitors' books and stamps.

It cannot be stressed too much that when hunting for a letter box no damage must be done to its neighbourhood, no litter or disfigurements left.

What follows is a list of the principal boxes.

Cranmere Pool (Grid reference 603858). Box faces east across the peaty hollow. Established by James Perrott in 1854. In Okehampton firing area.

Fur Tor (588830). In fissure on SW side of main rocks. Established c 1951 by Junior Leaders Regt, Royal Signals. In Okehampton firing area.

Crow Tor (606787). Under overhang of tor. Established 1962 by 2nd Christchurch (Twynham) Senior Scouts. In Merrivale firing area.

Ducks Pool (626679). Under large isolated rock on SE side of pool half mile east of Great Gnat's Head. Established 1938 by Dobson's Moormen, a Plymouth group of walkers, with plaque on rock to memory of William Crossing, who died 1928. Southern Dartmoor's rival to Cranmere.

Belstone Tors (613918). c 1900, exact position kept secret.

High Willhays (580893). In Okehampton firing area.

Lints Tor (580875). In Okehampton firing area.

Teign Head (617834). On E side of North Teign. In Okehampton firing area.

Flat Tor (604807). Established 1973 by Exeter University students in memory of Robert Burnard and William Crossing. In Merrivale firing area.

Fox Tor (626698).

Cuckoo Rock (585687). Isolated rock W of Combeshead Tor. No rubber stamp.

Fish Lake (647681). In tinners' hut beside tributary of Avon. Established by 21st Plymouth Scouts.

Grant's Pot (628670). Underground site on W side of the Wollake.

Hen Tor (594654). 9th Plymouth Scouts.

Appendix 4

	feet	metres
Bagga Tor, S of Standon Hill	1,219	372
Beacon Rocks, NW of Wrangaton	1,233	373
Bellever Tor, SW of Postbridge	1,456	444
Belstone Tor, S of Belstone	1,568	477
Brent Hill, N of South Brent	1,017	310
Brentor	1,130	344
Buckland Beacon, E of Buckland-in-the-Moor	1,282	391
Cawsand Beacon, S of Sticklepath	1,799	548
Cox Tor, NE of Tavistock	1,452	443
Crockern Tor, N of Two Bridges	1,295	395
Cut Hill, centre of northern wilderness	1,980	604
Eylesbarrow, E of Burrator	1,491	454
Fur Tor, NW of Cut Hill	1,876	572
Hameldown Beacon, NW of Widecombe-in-the-Moor	1,697	517
Hangingstone Hill, E of Cranmere	1,983	604
Haytor	1,491	454
High Willhays, S of Okehampton	2,038	621
Kestor, W of Chagford	1,432	436
King Tor, W of Princetown	1,314	401
Laughter Tor, NW of Dartmeet	1,409	429
Links Tor, Great, NE of Lydford	1,908	581
Mis Tor, Great, NE of Merrivale	1,761	537
North Hessary Tor, W of Princetown	1,695	517
Penn Beacon, N of Cornwood	1,407	429
Pew Tor, N of Sampford Spiney	1,051	320
Rippon Tor, SSW of Hay Tor	1,531	467
Ryder's Hill, S of Hexworthy	1,690	515
Sheepstor	1,150	351
Shell Top, N of Cornwood	1,546	471
Staple Tor, N of Merrivale	1,482	452
Stenga Tor, SW of High Willhays	1,900	579
Three Barrows, NW of South Brent	1,522	463
Ugborough Beacon	1,233	376
Vixen Tor, S of Merrivale	1,060	323
Yes Tor, S of Okehampton	2,030	619

Appendix 5

Dartmoor National Park Authority

A visit to Parke, the Bovey Tracey headquarters of the Park Authority, or any one of the seven outlying Information Centres, opens one's eyes to the tremendous work the Authority does. It not only looks after Dartmoor, but also takes great care in looking after visitors.

Statistics from the latest annual report give some clue to the scale of the work: over 200,000 visitors to the information centres, £500,000 income from sale of publications, 5,764 taking part in the 518 guided walks. The number of walkers has fallen by half since 1978 but this may well mean that more and more people are learning about the Moor and can walk independently.

The range of publications is tremendous and all-embracing. All serious visitors should obtain – free – *The Dartmoor Visitor* which in tabloid newspaper form gives a remarkable amount of information and help, from accommodation guidance to advice. For the motorist there is the *What to See from Dartmoor's Main Roads* which covers the two cross-Moor roads. For the walker there is a pocket folding card, *Comfort and Safety on Dartmoor*, which everyone should have, and the guided walk booklets are clear, informative and even have 2½in maps included.

Information Centres

Dartmoor National Park Authority headquarters, Parke, Haytor Road, Bovey Tracey TQ13 9JQ. Telephone No Bovey Tracey (0626) 832093.
Steps Bridge, New Bridge, Postbridge, Tavistock, Princetown, Okehampton and Buckfast.

Information Boards

Containing details of places to stay, places to eat and local services, available night and day. Located at Buckfast, Chagford, Dartmeet, Moretonhampstead, New Bridge, Postbridge, Widecombe, Ashburton, Buckfastleigh, Dunsford and Manaton.

Ranger Service

There is a Head Ranger and Assistant Ranger, and seven Rangers with districts of the Moor assigned to them. Their names and telephone numbers can be found in *The Dartmoor Visitor*.

Photographing Dartmoor

by Roy Westlake ARPS

This is a book of photographs of Dartmoor, but what is the real Dartmoor and why does it have such an irresistible appeal to so many people?

True it's a wilderness, but much of the surface has been turned over and rent apart by man in search of minerals. Old mine workings, now softened by age, are part of the scene.

Prehistoric man left his mark in stone rows, kistvaens and hut circles. For hundreds of years travellers have been guided across the open moor by granite crosses, and packbridges carried the same travellers across fast-flowing rivers. Most memorable of all are nature's weathered granite tors, distinctive, unique and timeless.

Dartmoor can be a bleak and inhospitable place, a land of sudden mists and squalls, uncomfortable – even dangerous – if not treated with respect. So why does it draw walkers like a magnet?

What brings teams of youngsters from all over the country to compete in the annual Ten Tors expedition? What prompts sensible adults to leave the comfort of their fireside and television to trudge from tor to tor looking for rubber stamps in old ammunition boxes? And why are the walks organised by the Dartmoor National Park Authority so popular, with groups following-my-leader across bogs and rivers to look at a tumbled mass of stone representing an old mine working, or a long line of irregular stones erected in the long distant past.

The answer must be a mixture of curiosity and challenge, deep seated instincts in all of us. Coupled with a child-like wonder of what lies over the next hill. Perhaps too the wish to escape from our well ordered television and computer dominated existence in home and office. To feel the wind in our faces and to look across open ground to distant landscapes.

Add to this the thrill of high places, the pleasure of solitude, or – depending on mood – the companionship of fellow walkers.

Now how do we attempt to capture on film this evocative atmosphere of the moor? In trying to interpet the varying moods and changing seasons we accept a considerable photographic challenge. Dartmoor is not an easy place to photograph, but the rewards can be great. Here are a few practical tips gleaned over many years of moorland walking.

There was an old saying amongst press photographers that the formula for a good picture was 'F8 and Be There'. F8 because this was the lens aperture most likely to give a printable picture under all conditions. Be there, the picture won't wait! This applied to the hurly burly of press work but, being in the right place, at the right time, with the right camera, is just as important in landscape photography.

When out walking always carry your camera. Lighting conditions do not wait and often there are only a few seconds in which to snatch a picture before the scene changes and that particular image has gone for ever. Be patient, but also be prepared to act quickly.

Landscape photography is largely selective. The photographer has little control over the scene; he can only find the best position, select the best lens and wait – and wait – for the lighting effect that he wants.

The best atmospheric pictures are usually to be found early in the morning, before the first rays of the sun have had a chance to destroy delicate shades of mist, or crisp frost. Taking against the light gives softer colours and increased contrast. It also dramatises features such as stone crosses.

The best colours are in the autumn, but don't neglect the heather and gorse of late summer. High summer is pleasant for walking, but the lighting is flat and hills tend to be featureless. Dramatic skyscapes are most likely in early winter when most sensible people are off the moor and tucked up by their fireside. It is then you will find the dedicated landscape photographer huddled under a tor sheltering from the bitter wind and waiting for a certain lighting effect on a distant hill. Cloud shadows can be used to emphasise the shape and contour of hills. Winter brings a beauty all its own, but do treat the moor with respect. Always go out equipped for bad weather, as well as photography. Warm clothing is essential – you may need to stand around.

Under storm conditions higher shutter speeds are necessary and do watch out for the danger of being blown off a high place while looking through the viewfinder. When getting out of a warm car in frosty conditions don't forget that the lens will mist over for a while.

Don't – as the author has often been guilty of doing – linger on the moor for one last shot when a storm is brewing, a blizzard about to dramatise the scene, or you can see the beginnings of a real Dartmoor mist which will nicely soften distant hills and separate the planes. Don't wait until your hands are too frozen to operate the shutter – or more importantly – to unlock your car door.

The softer perimeter is the ideal place for summer pictures, with numerous 'thatch and whitewash' villages, flower filled hedgerows and all the activities of the farming community to photograph.

Although the majority of these pictures were specially taken for this book, the remainder have been obtained over a number of years. All have given great pleasure in the taking. Cameras has varied from a very old Zeiss Ikonta to 35mm Canon and 2¼" square Hassleblad. All have their uses.

'Nowhere, perhaps, are the effects of light and shadow so striking as on Dartmoor. At times a distant hill is seen bathed in sunshine, while others in the foreground lie sombre beneath the clouds. Or we walk in the full glow of the sun below some lofty height which thrusts itself up into the gloom, looking frowningly on the golden world below. One side of a valley will smile in the brightness of a summer day; the other is grey and chill.'

WILLIAM CROSSING:
Gems in a Granite Setting

Leather Tor from Sheep's Tor.

LEFT
Sun breaking through early morning mist on Burrator Lake.

RIGHT
Ducks Pool nowadays contains little water. It is a marshy hollow in the centre of the Southern Moor, sought for its 'letter box'. Seen here under blue skies, it is a very different place in the depths of the winter.

LEFT
Early morning sun highlights dew on trees at Burrator.

RIGHT
The Tavistock Canal winds gently through pleasant countryside with mature trees lining much of its route.

Snow outlines the stark trees near Ringmoor Down.

Ice-encrusted grass makes a sparkling
pattern alongside the waterfall at Raddick
Hill on the Devonport Leat.

LEFT
The magic of autumn mists on the River Tavy,
near Denham Bridge.

ABOVE
Ponies seeking shelter from the rigours of the
open moor are clearly depicted against the
light.

LEFT

The scattered remains of Eylesbarrow mine workings stand out in sharp relief in the strong late afternoon sunlight. Sheep's Tor can be seen in the far distance.

RIGHT

Childe's Tomb (in fact, a kistvaen with a cross), in an isolated spot near Fox Tor, well known for its legend of Childe the Hunter.

LEFT
Sunset on the River Plym at Cadover Bridge.

RIGHT
*Looking from Peekhill, towards
Walkhampton Church.*

LEFT
In a winter setting, two desolate trees stand exposed against the skyline near Peekhill.

ABOVE AND BELOW
The chill of a winter's day in Dartmoor's woodlands.

Nun's (or Siward's) Cross is probably about 900 years old. It makes a dramatic – and useful – landmark on the Southern Moor.

'_And when the visitor, leaving the borderland, penetrates into the wild region, the conviction will be forced upon him that he is wandering through a domain of Nature altogether unlike any other that England can show._'

WILLIAM CROSSING:
A Hundred Years on Dartmoor

Wistman's Wood, in the valley of the West Dart, is believed to be more than 300 years old. Trees and boulders are mixed in utter confusion, with moss and lichen covering all.

LEFT

A gnarled tree in the churchyard of St. Michael of the Rock, Brentor, bears witness to the wild winds which sweep this exposed hilltop site.

RIGHT

Black-a-ven Brook, near Rowtor.

ABOVE
*This desolate scene is on the wide expanse of
the Northern Moor, near West Mill Tor.*

LEFT
*A winter tapestry, looking from Black Down
towards Nattor and the high moor.*

A last glint of sunshine before the storm, in Tavy Cleave.

Widgery Cross on Brat Tor silhouetted against strong sunlight.

On Kingsett Down, near Mary Tavy,
horses canter across a snow covered
landscape, in a study of freedom and
motion.

LEFT
Postbridge Clapper Bridge, on the East Dart River.

RIGHT
Fernworthy Reservoir covers some seventy six acres and is a good source for pictures. Here clouds reflect nicely in its still waters.

Lydford Castle.

'I oft have heard of Lydford Law,
How in the morn they hang and draw,
And sit in judgement after – – –.

A castle with an evil reputation for ill
treatment of those accused of offenses against
Stannary Laws.

Okehampton Castle, now a romantic ruin, is
in a commanding position above the West
Okement River. In its time it was regarded as
the strongest castle between Exeter and
Launceston.

ABOVE AND BELOW
Walkers in a heavy snowstorm are eventually rewarded with this view of the open moor, near Ger Tor.

RIGHT
Belstone Cleave is a steep sided well-wooded valley with several footpaths through its rock-strewn length.

* There are few greater contrasts than that exhibited by the desolate Moor and the fruitful valleys by which it is encircled. And this at once strikes the beholder, who finds his way to one of its frontier hills. On one side he sees fertility; on the other side barrenness. On this hand farms and villages that speak of the labours of man; on that a wide waste which shows few signs of his intrusion. 9*

WILLIAM CROSSING:
Gems in a Granite Setting.

LEFT

Typical of almost any river on Dartmoor after a heavy fall of rain. In fact, this is the Black-a-ven Brook again on the Northern Moor.

RIGHT

Tunhill Rocks, looking towards Wind Tor.

LEFT
The unmistakable outline of Bowerman's Nose, standing out on the skyline.

RIGHT
A squally day produces fine cloud effects. Looking from Hound Tor towards Cripdon Down.

Lower Cherrybrook Bridge. Icicles and snow epitomise winter on Dartmoor.

From the top of Haytor Rocks a magnificent view unfolds below.

LEFT
A picture full of autumn colour as the sun glints through golden leaves near Spitchwick, on the River Dart.

RIGHT
The 15th century church and green at Manaton. A peaceful place to sit and watch the world go by.

As clouds scud across the sky their shadows give shape to the hills around Widecombe-in-the-Moor.

Grey skies reflected in wind-swept water add drama and atmosphere to this view of Kennick Reservoir.

A dull misty day serves to emphasise the bleak location of Grimspound Bronze Age settlement.

LEFT
On Trendlebere Down, looking towards Pullabrook Wood.

RIGHT
Becky (or Becka) Falls have been popular since Victorian times. Here they are seen at their best, rich in autumn colour and with water flowing over tumbled rocks.

Widecombe-in-the-Moor church has been called the 'Cathedral of the Moor'. Its impressive 120 foot high tower makes it a prominent feature for miles around.

Bowerman's Nose is less than half that height, but it is another dominant feature on the skyline.

This picture of Wreyland Manor, which dates from 1389, must serve to epitomise all the snug 'thatch and whitewash' villages of this part of the moor – Lustleigh, North Bovey, Buckland and others.

Blackingstone Rock, a tor-like island in a sea of fields and woods, has superb views in all directions.

'Beautiful as Dartmoor is beneath a clear sky, and however inviting to the rambler it may then be, it is on a dull day that its wild grandeur becomes most impressive. We all love to look upon the sea of heather with the blue alone above it, but if we would know what the old Forest truly is we must seek it when clouds obscure the sun and its radiant mask is laid aside.'

WILLIAM CROSSING:
Gems in a Granite Setting

RIGHT
The view from Bench Tor along the Dart Valley is superb at any time; here storm clouds threaten and add drama to the scene.

LEFT
Huccaby (or Hexworthy) Bridge on the West Dart River. Hexworthy was a favourite of William Crossing and he often stayed near here.

RIGHT
The O Brook tumbles down its rocky channel near Saddle Bridge.

Combestone Tor is a rugged outcrop, easily accessible. It gives fine views of the Dart Valley in both directions, and of the open moor beyond.

A great day for walking the moor; clouds scudding across the sky, shadows constantly changing, a fresh wind, all contributing to a scene full of atmosphere. Near Bench Tor.

ABOVE
Vennford Reservoir has the purely mundane purpose of supplying the Torbay area with water. Yet when the light is right it can be a place of great beauty.

LEFT
The deep wooded valley of the River Dart.

LEFT
A group of walkers pauses for a 'coffee stop' on a fine spring day near Mel Tor.

RIGHT
In stark contrast, a winter scene at Sharp Tor a short distance away.

LEFT
Leigh Tor affords a panoramic view of the Dart Valley, here looking towards New Bridge, Holne.

RIGHT
Dartmeet Bridge, quiet in early autumn, seen from the hillside above.

'A stream catches the rays shot from an unclouded sky, and the ripples on its surface break into a thousand pieces; it glides towards a ledge of rocks, and falls into a deep hollow which is ever in shade, and becomes dark and sullen.'

WILLIAM CROSSING:
Gems in a Granite Setting

LEFT AND ABOVE
Two moods of the River Avon below the dam and near Shipley Bridge. The first, on a summer's day – caught so aptly in Crossing's words. In the second, it is transformed into a raging torrent after a heavy storm on the open moor.

FAR LEFT
The Avon Dam and Reservoir with a colourful foreground. In the background, the bleak moorland stretches far into the distance.